VIGIL

New Issues Poetry & Prose

Editor   Herbert Scott

Copy Editor   Curtis VanDonkelaar

Managing Editor   Marianne Swierenga

Assistant to the Editor   Kim Kolbe

New Issues Poetry & Prose
The College of Arts and Sciences
Western Michigan University
Kalamazoo, MI 49008

An Inland Seas Poetry Book

 Inland Seas poetry books are supported by a grant from
The Michigan Council for Arts and Cultural Affairs.

First Edition, 2006.

ISBN-10   1-930974-64-7 (paperbound)
ISBN-13   978-1-930974-64-7 (paperbound)

Library of Congress Cataloging-in-Publication Data:
Long, Alexander
Vigil/Alexander Long
Library of Congress Control Number: 2006924619

Art Director   Tricia Hennessy
Designer   Ben Bowes
Production Manager   Paul Sizer
                      The Design Center, School of Art
                      College of Fine Arts
                      Western Michigan University

VIGIL

ALEXANDER LONG

New Issues

WESTERN MICHIGAN UNIVERSITY

In Memory of W. F. & M. H.

Contents

I.

II.

III.

Acknowledgments

Thank you to the editors of the following journals and magazines where these poems first appeared, sometimes in different versions:

Askew: "Ode to Bombs"; "Elegy for a Love Poem I Meant to Write"

Blackbird: "The Gazing Eye Falls through the World"; "Regrets Only, Not Much"

Box Car Poetry Review: "Reading Whitman"; "Again"

Montserrat Review: "St. John's Extract"

Philadelphia Stories: "Unfinished Love Poem"

Pleiades: "Over the Orchards of Selma"; "Photograph: Anne Sexton on the Dust Jacket of Her *Complete Poems*"

Poetry International: "Night Sky"

Snake Nation Review: "After Meeting Muhammad Ali at Martini's Pizza Shop, Kalamazoo, Michigan, February 1998"; "Berryman"

I would like to thank Chris Buckley for his practical advice and invaluable support, Fleda Brown for crucial editorial suggestions, Bill Olsen for his faith in my work, and my many friends who've helped shaped this book. Very special thanks to my family, who've kept me afloat. Many thanks to Marina.

On the threshold of heaven, the figures in the street
Become the figures of heaven . . .

—Wallace Stevens

I.

Unfinished Love Poem

—for James Wright

Like I've been saying
All along, I'm not sure
Where they've gone
Off to. Why can't I think
Of that place as full
Of lovers secretly kissing
In unmodified light?
This afternoon's rain settles
Along my jaw.
I hope my bus is late.
Three beers by noon,
And now I go to chop
The rows of onions
For my bosses who mark
Up the booze for us all.
We keep coming back.
This is the life I've got.
I make salads from hearts
Of iceberg picked by migrants
Who curse and bless
This country, state, and town;
Their corner with the motel
Whose windows acquire a sheen
Over them as they drink
Five-dollar Cuervo
And spit it into their hands
To slick back their hair,
Desiring the unattainable
Strippers who pass through
Once a month. Sweet
Jesus, I keep imagining
The regulars and the lawyers drunk
Again, sliding off their chairs.

What I really like
About the clearest days
Isn't the light itself.
At the trolley stop in Sharon Hill,
Where I grew up and most can't
Leave, I'd stand there
With the two bums,
Big Bob and Chicken Man.
For being desolate, they dressed
Nice. They stank, though,
And sniffed glue every chance
They could. Otherwise,
They no longer seemed to desire a thing,
Not even the other's shadow
On the hottest afternoons, flirting
With oblivion, waving to it
As it floated by quiveringly
Over their ears,
White and light as milkweed.
Trying to think of them again,
In their polyester suits
And dress shirts
Buttoned all the way up
To their scruffed wattles,
Whose collars resembled a hit pigeon
I saw once by the curb—
Its wings lifting slightly
As another A. Duie Pyle rig
From Pittsburgh barreled through
Sharon Hill, where I grew up,
Without stopping until it hit
The limits of West Philly—
I can see they have
Completed that agenda the dead
Stars have laid out, and I don't know

Where they are now. So it is
This bus stop
We all end up at,
Telephone wires swaying
Between oceans, the sun
Hovering right there, between
Our fingers, with all its busted light.
I've heard it called a lot
Of things, not one of them
Accurate. The pines
And maples dripping with rain,
For example, have their Latin
Names that make them
Seem larger, which I can remember
Well enough most days,
Which I love.

After Meeting Muhammad Ali at Martini's Pizza Shop, Kalamazoo, Michigan, February, 1998

> *He's too ugly to be the champ. Look at me, I'm pretty.*
> —Muhammad Ali

What needs to happen now
Has little to do with accuracy,
Or the mesmerization we feign
For all the obvious reasons
Regarding his single force:
A magic trick that ends
In his quivering left fist
Holding a linen napkin
That flutters like the resignation
Of a touched butterfly.
Let me remind you
That our subsequent applause
May invoke the old imprecations—
"I am the greatest of *all* time;
What's my name? What's my name!"—
Even as the children continue
To approach, as he hugs them
For so long that we begin to sway
A little with them, forgetting
That our distance is still
An exile from the first love.
If I could stake my claim
For once on the future tense,
Where the stars refuse to emerge
From the orange-flamed horizon
To which we are attached,
Where geometry will not soften
For even God the Man,
We would, with all our overdue respect,
Approach him with our hats and gloves

In one hand, and extend our other,
To shake his hand,
To tremble because of him,
And with him.

It's Tuesday

—for William Matthews

I've had a soft pretzel
                    a little stale
With salt
           brave little stones
Dissolving in my blood
                   racing my heart
Among the other things

And mustard
              the color of a hayfield
Miles from here
            untouchable
Mostly because it's there
And you're
        say
             here

That's the plan

And elsewhere hydrangeas tilt
Toward the sun
              whose real beauty lies
Under ground

You know well
           what I'm talking about

In two hours I'll have that cigarette

That's the plan
            timed rewards

Taking care
                like the time you read

And read well
                from *Time & Money*

A big hit
                out everywhere

Later to The Bar with big exotic fish
In tanks
                poor stunned cousins

All of us with our faces pressed
Up against one barrier
                        of light
Or another

And bombshell waitresses
                        stalling a bit

Your wit
        diamonds
                of rage and love

My drinking
Extravagant tipping
                Nothing more

Cheaply acquired

Up and down the long tables
And bottles of wine

All chummy by then
                    and you ran out
Of Reds and me
                to the rescue

Here take two they're Lights

Lit up
        moved on
                    to Scotch

Were asked to leave
                    and lock the door

Blind faith

I'll show you around New York kiddo
It doesn't close

In two hours
                a cigarette

Still Tuesday
            you say

I figured

Just checking

Berryman

Here we are again,
This puddle, this meek wind,
This swaying sycamore,
The sky unfettered
Inside it all.
John, I think
It would have been better
If you jumped
From the Whitman—
One poet leaping
Off the memory of another
And straight into Jersey.
Maybe we should be singing
"Eleven Addresses to the Lord"
To ourselves, but I'm going
To see you wave
To the cars
As you stand
On the pedestrian walk
Of the Whitman
In a Phillies cap,
White breath frozen
Into that beard of yours—
Oh I love how you've let it go—
Slush sprayed up to your shins
And soaking your socks,
Sorrow running
Through you, meeting
At your heart in a bad duet
Of blood and alcohol.
You must be freezing,
The wind whipping
Through your ears and hands

As faint as a little boy
Coughing into his shirt sleeve
At the top of a sycamore.
I've got so much
Movement and color
In this puddle
I'm convinced
What you did was as plain
As these brittle tongues
Of frosty light.
I see myself
Shivering in and out.
It's hard at the bottom,
Or the surface, or whatever
The hell
It finally is.

Reading Berryman

The girl and her dog
Are the only ones left
                    in the park

Salt wind again
                not different
Not ever really
                from this chair
I've sat in for countable weeks

This is when I'm most fearful
                            unforthcoming

Vistas endured
                a bit
For the merciful Lord

Dusk as labial as fire

The dog's tongue draped to the side
Of his fangs
                the girl picking dandelions
Shooing leisurely from her ear a bug so

One could think she was waving *hello*

A Minute Ago I Was Reading Dickinson

Can you hear me today
                blank sheets all over the courtyard

Signifying wind and a minute ago
                      something purer

Of course
        wind doesn't blow as its movement

Is and in so doing transparent
                obvious

Enough like phonics
             right
                and by extension rhyme and by extension

You
      lost and lost on me sometimes
                      a double loss sometimes except

To know this is to come closer to naming
                      the mind behind hawks' bones
For instance
        groove and joint and joint and groove
                      and no marrow i.e.

God as a silk spool
             no deadly
              like a spool of silk

Or deadly as the sound of silk becoming a shirt by hand
                      slipped on then off
So one can see what moves one so
             slowly through

Narrative threads all over the courtyard on the backs of blank sheets

Like a picture of me in that blue little row boat

I don't want to explain it and now I have to

Feet not touching the sea and behind me

1976 maybe
         maybe Atlantic City
                  city of lights clicking on the horizon
Of space
        space neighboring the ocean's horizon

Whole messes of cosmoses
            that loaded gun
                 over my shoulder
                     way out there

It haunts me some to hear the waves departing like grace
                 or childhood

Still it must have been a pretty afternoon

Whoever took the picture must have said *right here sailor*
                 because I am

Photograph: Anne Sexton on the Dust Jacket of Her *Complete Poems*

11 A.M. late spring in Boston

For years sun and wind and dust
                              in the corner
Of my eyes I don't feel

The coffee only warm and matches
Meat-red tips exposed
                         sliced fingers
Salems in their soft pack waiting to burn

The typewriter loaded
                      and you are
All this beauty at your desk
Shoes on
            arms and legs bent
Like open scissors held up
By your left wrist

You are lovely

I was hoping you would be
                           wrapped
In a peach robe running your hands
Through your hair
                      Bloody Mary and cigarette streaming
From the ashtray
                   perhaps too easy

Last night we had Manhattans in bed
                              I remember
Muttering something as we danced

You like Monk's covers
Of Ellington best?

You went on and on
                    to my ear with your tongue again

Then morning

I've held your perfume and cigarette breath
On my collar
              I don't need to say that
I want to be this photographer
And stop a little time

As you take a deep drag and blow
That damaged air into me

So your breath might swim awhile

Like the sweet weight of birds inside you
Like this darkened favored light that covers you

Reading Whitman

I've been dying my whole life
                        who hasn't

To get to someplace
                        if not New Orleans then at least

A party where costumes are preferred

Showing the wicked bodies' argument against the earth like this

The standard stuff
                        heels and fishnets and all that beauty pushed up

Lavender boas and black bras
                        did I say whose

Tongue that was
                        out of hope whose tongue and ear that was that was

Loving her body's wicked arguments against an earth like this

Ragweed and milkweed
                        blithely scattered and suburban lawns

Would do if she will for a spread bed
                        where her arm is thrown across the sky

On the surface languidly so and still utterly
                        surrounded by stars

Showing our bodies' wicked argument against their earth like this

And like this
            my settled head athwart her hips if she wants me to

So it's been written and duly stolen
                        so inside too hummingbirds' blood pumps

A tachycardia iambic
            through all zones slender and wide that I'll let run awhile

My body's wicked argument against the earth like this

Again

No one is sleeping.
—Lorca

You tap the naked light
Bulb and blink. The second
Of October, nineteen
Twenty-nine, 6 A.M.
A trolley car clanks, squeals;
The silver spigot trickles;
Your unopened mail holding
News from Granada,
Of Franco, sits on the trunk
Like certain photographs.
You know seventy-five years
From now, a man will sit
Down on this very day
To try to step into
Your day, just as you are
About to step into
Whitman's, the New York
He lost and sang; New York
Of statistics and columns,
Police and perfume, frozen
Rivers of silver
And cement, seething
Rivers of lament and tar.
In seven years, you will
Die on a road without
A name, and crows will claim
You as their own, a bullet
In your back and a boot
Print on your cheek. In seven
Times seven times seventy
Years, you will visit
New York again and hold
Whitman's hand, and in

That moment when 6 A.M.
Is 6 P.M., when his
Hand is your hand, you will
Broadcast depressions
And offer yourselves
To the empty offices
You walk through this last time
Forever. But really,
It's only now and who
Will ever earn enough
To lick dirt from your boots, souls?
So you walk dark halls,
Down stairs, into the street.
You become the herding,
Coughing crowds of those looking
For work, for time to speed up
And slow down, a little
Light, like the man sitting
Here with you in his gray breath,
Though he doesn't yet have
The full-noon words to begin
Breathing them again.

Reading Levis

And even the language he used to explain it all
Is dying a little more, each moment, as I write this—
                    —Larry Levis

Perhaps a name is given to be
                   lost
                         nothing more

Whether said or scrawled or both

It's gone and pristine

Don't say a word

So as not to break from this

Landscape where one apple will not be
Mildewed from a little girl's breath

The breath of someone I can't find a name for

Or a photograph that has for a background
An intersection
                  in Fresno twenty years later

The Dominguez Brothers in the foreground
Sitting on the bed of a pickup
                      whose make and model escape me

I can't see them
           still
                after all this time

Never have
                but they're there

Which is to say they've
                        gone off to where

Better still to say it and break from it

Gone   Off   To

She is somebody too
                let's say their sister

This little girl who's done nothing but breathe and stare
At her veiled reflection in a stupid little apple
After she's polished it with her pajama sleeve

Look at her a long time is all I'm asking
And do your best to keep your mouth shut

It will be dark but you can have a moon if you're good

You can put it wherever you want if you're good

Mine is going on her pajamas a hundred times
                                    and as she turns to sleep   31
Her arm dangles off the side of the bed
                                her hand
Sort of resembling tulips slumped with a little rain inside them

She stays there as long as the alphabet

concocts light
And hear her breathing
　　　　　　that's the sound of stone
Suspending the only judgment it's been afforded

But I'll pass this on to you
　　　　　　and like I said keep quiet and it'll be all yours

Hear me

　　　*　　　*

As if there were another way to put it

As if there were another way for it to happen
　　　　　　　she dies

Six months later on the way to the emergency room in Angel's arms

He was running with her in his arms
　　because their pickup wouldn't turn over

There's always a reason or whatever
　　　　　　you want to call it
And there's always a name for those left
　　　　　　behind　.

For Johnny and Angel her shape

                              at the kitchen table
Drinking milk from a mug the size of her head

For Johnny and Angel the way things happen
    are the way things happen

What did you expect
                    Philosophy   Theory   Elegy

Her name is Rosa Luna Dominguez and you don't get it on a stone

And neither do Johnny and Angel because there is no because

Silver Rose or
            White Rose or
                        Rising White Moon or

White Rose Rising Over the Blazonry of Princes or
                                    Rosie or

Over the Orchards of Selma

—*for Larry Levis*

I'm listening for the music of elegant Spanish
Insults from your father's grape gleaners,

Johnny and Angel, for dust

To crackle over Vivaldi on vinyl
In your father's dark room,

For the chants of girls
Outside because I can't help it.

It's the rhythm I like. "We all fall down,"
Sings to me now, sweetly

As Monk's pinky commanding
The clouds to part

Through a simple pressing of keys. *God damn*
It all is what my father

Would bellow. I'd come home,

Four in the morning, doors
Slamming, birds singing.

He couldn't help it.

He listened for me.
This was our pact,

Congealing the blood. That's all

There is to sleep on. I'd like to
Join those girls, talk

Until someone listens,

To their father with the bat,
Whisper in his ear that it's possible

To make a bat's grain confess
The sorry incongruities of the gnostics

If you're ever going to have a good time,
And find your way home.

Instead, I'm off to McGlinchy's
To toast your wren

Who flew backwards into eternity

As a poem, and made it.

We'll break and sink
Nine-ball. Those who smoke

Can, those who need to call home
Should. We'll call out from work,

We'll call out over the orchards of Selma,

Their white flags, as if there were something
To surrender to, singing

"Cielito Lindo" as long as we can
Stand it, as long as our cracked

And cracking voices,
Like the rotting angels

We are, will let us.

II.

Night Sky

—after Vallejo

A clear, cool night—as the *Times* predicted.
Sleep will come if I lay my head and listen
To the waves departing again like childhood.

Yes, sleep will come if I stare long enough
Toward the floodlit lot and black steel of the fire
Escape where two teenagers, kissing, feel something

I've forgotten the name of. Above their almost
Endless kissing, an entire nation of fireflies
Scatters its affection as light over asphalt.

Sunday still. Black stone sky that fills each hour,
Let it rain—it's so predictable. My yellow bones
Sing the wrong notes, it hurts some, but I listen.

Everything was possible once from that old table
Where I sat drawing shapes of asphodel and ash—
So, tell me, again, that your elegy will be rain, a poem

Of fireflies and waves washing the bodies of gulls
And lost fathers in casual swells onto the shore
Of your one and only sea, one voice making straight

And slow the path of time. No matter, I will be
Right here on a Sunday, a Sunday like this one,
Dusk-light like shimmied water blanching the alley

Into a kind of parchment, the windows staring,
The lines of laundry swaying then straightening,
Hissing lazily as they do . . . and there on the fire

Escape, the boy with the red hat, that's me, once,
With a longing for distance, more or less. More
Or less, Alexander Long is dead—he's been sitting

Out here all night thinking there would be time,
Which is also here, undulating like the shadows
Of steam rising from his coffee, and the *Times*

Carefully folded on the small table. No one hated him,
The blurb might say, though he seemed to ignore them
As he sat shaded by the poplars, reading, his lips

Moving for someone perhaps he couldn't quite see
Yet, or simply something, with practice, he chose
To ignore. Inside the *Times*, more weather that will

Surely come, sudden-death victories and predictable
Vacancies, ink on the cloud-dull paper, flesh becoming
Words beneath the quiet demarcations of the rain.

Ode to Bombs

I'm thinking that whistling far off in the distance
                                                    there
Is something to hum along with. It's history's
                                                    little anthem,

And we hum its one note as long as we can breathe
It through, don't we . . . .
                                        And when the whistling stops,

There's no city of fire, no blackened glass,
                                                    no girders

Curved around and through the village's last and useless horse.

There's only a story, the truest one, that no one
                                                    tells, or can.

So, go on, drop
                    the landscape into tidily shattered lines that drop
                                                            themselves,

Then, look up
                    at clouds that neither gather nor hover,

But simply are, are scattering from smoke,
                                                are almost celebrating
                                                    themselves,   41

Their invisible, inevitable dissolution,

As the planes go on bestriding each other,

And the glass, the girders, the horse, the village
                                                    let go

Of themselves, and why not? I'm thinking . . .
                                        I'm thinking

Ecstasy, a loss
                of breath, a hovering, some alley

In a corner of Baghdad where two teenagers

Feel each other up, and the whistles multiply and amplify,
                                                why not,

As a little fire
                spreads from home to home, and why

Not have the boy strike a match, which makes the girl
                                                giggle,

To light his cigarette, for this is the custom of adults . . . .

I'm thinking he calls her *Oh Donna* and *Runaround Sue,* and he
                                                        drags

And hums and breathes the smoke into her,
                                        where every thought
Is permissible and rebellious, and hums along,
                                        inaudibly,

Goodbye goodbye goodbye . . .

On Politics Being Personal

To write poetry after Auschwitz is barbaric.
—Theodor Adorno

I could begin with this fog's refusal
To burn, to tell the sun's entire story;

Or I could begin with this cigarette
And cup of coffee, which, every morning,

Never refuse to burn, to tell.

They help me forget these dreams
That bolt me awake.

Now, now, please don't think
This has anything to do

With the poet's burden of solitude,

Or of prize readings, handshakes and hugs,
Snide remarks over Manhattans,

The little cubes of cheese
And theory, white wine in plastic cups

As dry as a committee meeting.

Go on, chuckle, chortle, herr doktor.

Let the ice in your cup clink and sweat.

I wonder if I've ever cared. I used to feel
My poems would matter,

That they would lead me somewhere,
That they were as authentic

As, say, genocide, or that, somehow,
I might matter someday simply

Because I'd worked on a poem late
Into the next millennium, representing with all the salt

I could steal, those I loved and perhaps knew.

Now, I work late reading Adorno. Now, I know,
Like you, that these years of listening

Have come to this. Without trying,

Or by trying too hard, I've gotten lost. Enough
Confessions. I sip coffee

And shiver as fog rolls in. I breathe fire
Mixed with cloves, which kill, and have been killed

Over. I imagine her putting on icicle earrings.

I'd get lost in their little sway, the way
They dangled when she brushed a stray hair

From her cheek as she smoothed some rouge
Before she left for the hash and trance

Rooms at Club Roxy.

And now I can feel
Myself getting lost in her accent again,

Soft, throaty ks and lovs mingling
With black hair, blue eyes, and absinthe. I remember

Feeling something close, which I
Mistook for something fatal. Before

Each pause in her story, she would ask,

You see? or How you say?—not
To clarify, but to flirt a little,

Like I seem to be doing here with you.

I wanted to place each of her earrings
Into my mouth and let gravity do the rest,

Even as she told me about '89, when she
Was a student. In Prague, during the fall

(She said it with audible italics),

They called it "The Student Rebellion,"

And those who were still students
Linked arms with those who were no longer

Students and those who would never be
Students before they scattered down the alleys like floodwater.

And they ran from building to building,
Banged on windows and shouted

Sweet nothings, prepared to be shot

With tear gas and carried away in vans
That would never make it to Siberia.

It was only when she ran up the steps
Of Charles University and saw three Soviet soldiers

Sitting there smoking that she began to understand
Freedom. She saw the boredom and guilt

Etched into the lines of their faces.

She saw their rifles dangling like fishing rods.

And she imagined her cousin Jan
Hacking the Berlin Wall with a hammer, not

Because he was a hero, but because he was tripping

On mushrooms, because he felt something
Clawing him, something that would kill him

With deliberate slowness, and laughter,
Which eventually came true

In an institution south of Kiev.

She grabbed my wrist and squeezed until
It couldn't hurt anymore.

And then, she said, she felt a tremendous weight
Being draped over her, the weight of being

Alone for the first time in her own land,
No longer united in the abstractions

That promise suffering and redemption, a cause.

This was the first time
She understood what nothing felt like.

So let me tell you that her name is Erika,
Let me tell you that I believe

In her story. And like Erika, I will refuse,
At this point in the story, to tell the truth.

Not because she asked me to,
But because it feels

Like the right thing to do,

You see?

At the Movies

I am hypnotized by a distance . . .
                        —Roland Barthes

Is it that we're let in
                        one
By one through the lobby past
The plastic gods of leisure
                            we might still become
I bet
        water spinning from their hands and feet

Groping
            fondling
                    no smiles   blush

It's not that they let a kid tear my ticket and tell me where to go
His acne scrubbed raw
                        scars of stars along his temple

Is it
        but that I go and sit and wait

Chatting over the music tinctured
With fear and hope and all the love
                                that's slipped
Inside the coming attraction's trailers

As one light dims and another begins

And I've guessed all along
                        what would become
Of Roberto
            oh Roberto
                    his bicycle

The loaf of peasant bread with crust like tree bark

The road home lost in all that dust

That I too will move
                out and away
                            and biolytic as we all are

I will
        a small eon from now in Newark

Wave from across the hotel bar
                        offer to pick up whatever it is

The other is having
              I'm thinking we'd do

This a moment or two
               maybe longer

And still the *me* and the *thee*
                    different rooms and the twitching blue
Light of pay-per-view

I've got all kinds of love
            Love
          really

The Gazing Eye Falls Through the World

—for Ono No Komachi, 834-880 A.D.

Philadelphia, almost dawn. The Delaware stares
Back like lilies. In their ten thousand sets of eyes

A hawk's claw moon again, hung barely,

And there goes a train clearing snow
For someone beautiful. And while she isn't sure

Why, she's dreaming of moving again
While a Japanese poem whisks by in shapes the snow makes:

*As certain as color
Passes from the petal,
Irrevocable as flesh,
The gazing eye falls through the world.*

The heart does break.

Ono No Komachi did not beg for her beauty back
On the streets of Kyoto, and the boys running
Past her did not throw carp at her feet,

Nor did they force her to see her age anymore
Than she already had, for she was fire, only

Smarter. Yet, I exist, is the line she hides.

Her eyes, hazel if the sun glanced her face
As she turned away from the street and toward the sea,

Would tell it another way, distilling, as they had for years,
The Sea of Japan until it was a shawl draped across her back,

Its wind carrying the scent of a snuffed candle, until
She was a little snow drifting onto white paper

Containing no lines . . .

*   *

A stack of white paper, in fact, packed
In a box and taken cross-country.

Even if this story weren't true, I'd still tell it.

I traveled with a woman whose eyes reminded me of Komachi's,

And on a train stranded outside Strongsville, Ohio,
We held hands as long as we could.

The trees rustling lullabyed like waves.

I'm keeping this picture.

In another, the man—crack, angel dust, loss—who clicked the camera
Must have said *Smile Sweetie* because she is,

In one of those blue Nantucket chairs.

Her feet don't touch the grass, and behind us
An afternoon drifts

Into Michigan, a horizon of stains stirring
A song from a wren I used to be able to hear.

These kinds of epiphanies, friends, rise as blown snow,
As flame. The cosmos is trapped inside me,

And her, now, and her muffled laughter
Into my arm that day,

Her laughter and surprise mingling with pity

At the man shifting his legs and arms, looking
As though he were fretting an equation he couldn't factor

Into this last decade of his life, one failed attempt
At kicking after another,

How he almost moved in concert with things
Around him, with the august music of snow and Mozart

He could see from the high window of his room.

And now it's me fretting over that day when he held
The camera, zoomed us in, raised a finger, then pressed

The ball of his hand to his temple, the gesture
Of Aquinas flirting with confusion, only

To disappear into a fog covering all things
Worth glimpsing, as it always does, because

He had resumed his sermon, the one with no ending,
Whose ellipses carry the scent of ecstasy:

Sulfur of a snuffed flame and crystal-led breath
Blossoming by his heart.

He shook, briefly, and dropped the camera to the grass,

Indifferently as a dirty shirt, or notepad full of slant rhymes,
And sat under a dogwood.

She couldn't speak, so she laughed.

If laughter is a kind of music whose theme is forgetting,
Then I hear it transposing a temporary affliction,

Happiness, perhaps; belief

In an incalculable beauty of numbers;

The sound of her voice hailing a taxi to the airport.

*   *

And so once more the scene is full of perfect reminders,

Whatever form harmony decides not to take:

The Delaware carrying a baby carriage, wheels-up;

A rusted muffler pushed into its bank; and deeper still,

Her freckled forehead when she used to lean over me
As I napped in our yard, the past kissed and set spinning, even then . . .

And now . . . the searing bliss of the runner's high
I've learned to acquire, Sapphire gin on the rocks.

And the names we gave, the smallest stories
Of a flocculent sun that seemed to matter once:

Jelly Bean, Baby Man, Gloria & Zeus, Honey Suckle . . . .
I've tried to forget, and tried. In time,

I will, with practice, and extravagant, long-winded lists.

Still, they were all we had, so we held onto them,
Almost fiercely, and without any regard

For reality, whatever that may come to be.

Today, it's a river, snow in the form of words,
Me humming a Paul Desmond riff, for sadness

Gravitates toward other sadnesses.

Each night, after his third scotch, and feeling an air
Pearl-pure in his lungs, he'd light a Lucky, drag, then ride

The lowest B-flat his alto allowed.

The smoke grew from the bell like a lily,
Trickled through its keys,

And when he was done, streamed the rest
From his nose with a grunt.

This was triage for the soul, and while cancer transcribed itself
Onto his lungs, he could taste the purl of heaven,

Which came from the reed.

It burned a little and carried a hint of tobacco, maple wood,

And Glenlivet 18.

When he leaned over to kiss the girl he thought he saw and knew,
There was an empty space with lilac still lingering.

Actually, there were many,

Though their names became one drawn-out phrase
Whose root was in the key of loss,

Or B-flat. It's easy

To get lazy in a world like this, to let the shoulders slump
Under serenity's lassitude,

To let the eyes fall through it all, like light.

Near the end, she and I simply stopped listening
Because what we had to say amounted to a gesture

Of confused indifference:

A flick of hair over the shoulder, tapped ash, the head bent
Back, as though to climax, a throat

Opened and releasing its smoke, enhancing
And ending slowly all the rhythms of pleasure the body allows.

It takes a while to figure this.

It's meant to.

Good-bye anticipates both sides of nothing.

Elegy for the Dark Anniversaries

Who among the numberless you have become desires this moment

Which comprehends nothing more than loss & fragility & the
    fleeing of flesh?
He would have to look up at quickening dark & say: *Me. I do.*
    It's mine.

—Larry Levis

The cruelest are June,
Then May.
The imagination
Has a need
To inhabit that gauzy realm
Of the would- and
Should-have-beens.
This is ecstasy,
And this is how a life
Breaks down.
Let's put coyness
Over here,
Up high
On the shelves
Of history, inside
The *OED* and *DSM-IV,*
Press it
As one might
Press baby's breath
Into the Proverbs,
The Gospel of John.
I broke my life.
You know
The story,
Maybe
Heard it
Told in a voice
That could tease

Out as much
As it should
From style and loss,
From something
As shear and unbearable
As a summer dress.
There isn't a point, now,
In avoiding it.
I slipped it off
Of her, and weeks
Later, I married
Another woman.
This was June.
In May,
That voice I loved
Silenced itself, as all music does:
Too soon,
And left us
Wanting more.
He was young,
Enough, but
One of the late photos
Tells another story.
Slumped shoulders,
Streaks of white
Up top; gray along
The top of the lip;
Sleep dark, like ash,
Nests under his eyes.
Blurred in the background,
A row-home yard
In Richmond, Virginia
Or Selma, California.
I feel as though
I'm describing a body.

Maybe I am.
Hers was beautiful,
And when I looked
At what I'd uncovered,
She smiled, briefly,
Too. Afterwards,
We all concluded
That none of us was
In love. With anyone.
And so, over time,
We walked
Into our own slow vertigo,
Mainly with the assistance
Of lawyers,
And through the postal service.
I wish I knew
How it is
That I can walk
All day
Among strangers,
And say next to nothing.
At the Holocaust
Museum, you can walk
For hours and speak
To strangers
With your eyes,
Shoulders, and hands
That flip
Through an ID card
Of someone
"Permanently solved"
By the S.S.
It's a replica.
The originals bloom

As tulips and daffodils
In Lodz, Gdank,
Krakow, and will,
Some day,
In Montenegro,
Sudan, Mesopotamia.
Before you can
Step from the elevator
That leaves you
On the fourth floor,
A photograph
As wide as a wall
Greets you:
"American Troops Uncover
Bodies at Ordruf."
You know
This story, too,
And unlike other stories
I've told,
This one deserves
To be told again
In a voice
I've acquired
Through imitation,
the sincerest form . . . .
American GIs, waiting
For Eisenhower,
Didn't stumble
Upon the camps.
They were looking
For them,
And for prisoners.
When they found them,
A century,
Not yet half over, fell

Apart. Ten thousand
Pounds of hair,
Six hundred thousand
Sets of teeth,
And a millennium
Of bones bristling
Under the skin,
Which were wrapped,
And systematically unwrapped
By a desire
Historians have tried
To label *perverse,*
A word
Whose origins
Can be traced
Back to the Latin
Vertere or turn,
And *conversari,*
Or to live, a little
Conversation,
A communion,
And also
Converse,
A proposition or relation
Turned upside down.
The language

Of entropy
Is the entropy
Of language.
What else can follow
But a deep breath,
And anger, and a little
Relief? This
Is the kind of survival
Dr. Levi talks about,

The kind of survival
That finally hurls
Him down
A flight of stairs
With forty years
Of inexplicable,
Understandable
Guilt strapped
To his back.
He fell
So it would shatter.
This is memory
In bloom.
It is
A blue tattoo
On the left forearm,
A ring not on a finger,
Some crusts of bread
On a plate eaten
After one can't eat
Any more,
Out of habit,
And of reverence.
This is how a life
Is made.
At my wedding
Reception, a minister
Gave us grace
Before we sat to eat,
To celebrate
All we had
Lying before us.
We clasped
Our hands,
Bowed our heads,

And hummed *amen.*
What was it
We were thinking
Then? Outside,
Sun dusked the creek.
A dove mourned
Something. The roses
In her bouquet
Swelled with water
And light.
They'll make it,
She said, *at least*
Through the night.

Regrets Only, Not Much

1. "O Holy Night"

I would give almost anything to understand why
You threw the leftover wedding invitations we made by hand

Into the dumpster, and why, before you did it,
You kissed them. And how we argued for hours

Over the RSVP, what it really meant and the cost of it all.

It was beginning to freeze outside then, too. Not much,
But enough to remember it by.

And I would give anything to know why
The more I try to remember you away from that day,

The more I feel myself sliding toward you,
The more I hear the cracking of things.

Really, what cracks is the city, wind squeezing
Buildings, taxis and buses and rigs

Pressing down streets, shoppers bundled and huddled
Arm in arm, mouthing cold smoke

Of Christmas carols as they float from shop to shop:

Let nothing you dismay . . . oh what fun . . . fall on your knees . . . .

And your voice . . .
                              or my memory of it.

It's all the same, and I don't know where I go,
Really, when I slip into it.

Wherever it is, it's not far, but it is

unreachable. .

If I could hear your voice in a new way
As I step out into this newer cold

And watch my breath swim through bitter air
With carols streaming through snow beginning,

Would that make it better somehow?

Would I begin to forget, for example, how I
Laid you down to sleep, eased you

Into it for years with a cup of warm milk and a little tune

Your grandmother hummed?

There's more to pain than memory.

Besides, ours was another life, the one not set in type,
And if it were the only life, nothing

Would have happened between us.

       *   *

I'm barely thirty, and to talk about this is hard,

Not because of the pain,
But because I can't remember it enough, so tangled

And torn and fleeting, I feel the old love stirring:

Pleasure is hardly crueler than the memory of it.

So, Reader, stand here with me on this cold corner,
Just this once, toss your clumsy bags of gifts to the street,

Wrap your scarf around your chin, and look at this woman.
She's all we need to share.

She keeps waving cars down, yelling.
Not one stops. But they slow, seem to listen.

And look at the man with the long beard and camouflage coat,
The tattoos clawing around his neck, and his Doberman

Wrapped in a black smock and silver spiked muzzle,
How they move a little to the left, and then a little more.

Is it fear?
              She must be freezing as she turns

Into angry water, as her curses become the sharp, invisible crystal
That, if caught in something more than an image,

Would resemble oversized snowflakes,
The kind children make with paper and scissors.

It's gorgeous how that happens, don't you think?

The Doberman's breath as she curls around her master's feet,
The crystal streaming from her snout,

The man's shushes into her clipped ears,

The laughter of those on the street at the woman,
                                              or not,

The woman's cursing at what she sees,

or doesn't . . .

Their parade of white breath rising with the carolers' . . .
Cold, white, gone. Beautiful communion . . .

Jesus Christ with ice . . . . Hello, goodbye, and the stars
Are brightly shining . . .

I would give anything to understand why this happens, the marriage
Of breath and ice, strange couplings and shatterings

Ordained, then abandoned, by wind.

If there were a way I could hold it together,

I'd be writing something different,
A different kind of love poem, maybe, the kind

Sketched in crystal, one
I could hold you in, remember you enough by.

2. Kristallnacht

Much to their dismay, certain S.S. guards found female Dobermans
Superior. Their sense of smell was more acute,

More receptive to what we call terror,

Their ferocity more easily triggered by waving
A wolf's tongue dripping with their pups' blood

In front of their muzzled, spiked snouts.

Then, they'd be let loose to tear you
Into the crystallized breath you are becoming

Less and less of.

They would tear, and not let go.

And as you ran and jumped and cursed
Through the alleys of Dinslaken, Munich, Augsburg—

And later Warsaw, Paris, Prague—

Your screams, if your screams rang that far,
Would become as mute as the effigy

Of, say, Wagner glaring toward Moscow from the Charles Bridge,
The Vlatava rippling with Nazi U-boats,

Frozen along its banks, where, more than once,
A man and his grandson unsuccessfully fished.

As you told me this, you began to laugh
The kind of laugh that refuses to tell the entire story.

In your concealment, I began to understand.

There are things we choose not to say, and there are things
We cannot say simply, and these words,

You assured me, were not yours. They were your grandmother's.   67

And still are.

But the more I pay attention to what I remember, the more I slide
Into your laughter, into my own telling:

"How did we end up at Kristallnacht, anyway?
We were supposed to be breaking up . . . ."

I still wish I knew what to say. You were hushing
Yourself then because of the listeners, like I'm doing now,

       *   *

And as I think softly, I'm really speaking out loud.
About your voice, that is, and the sleet, and the windowpanes shining

With the ice. I can almost see you now behind that fogged window

Marinating chicken in a plastic container. Why?
                              No one else
Is home. It's been this way for years.

You stand at the counter, turning over and over
The meat, the sleet falls, and it's not much, you think.

The lawyers haven't called, haven't written, won't listen,

And it's not much. You mutter it softly, not much, not
Much, splintered iambs under your breath until you can't hear them

Anymore, even though you're speaking plainly above
A whisper by now, clearly above the stereo and Bourbon on the rocks

And Camel Lights, which float into their own rhythm, flaming—

not much, not much, not much

Echoing down halls we painted blue.
Ring, and after-ring, ice on glass, and echo again.

No one's coming home, not much not much not much,
And even here, Reader, the sleet begins to patter trochaically.

I know it's too much. I know. I know
                              it's been falling so
steadily

That it takes on a life of its own in world that unravels

Right next to ours, this world we know
Where meaning has been banished, where the only law

Is the freezing water of regret kissing sound.

Which means, I'm thinking, there is no law.
                              Listen—

Elegy for a Love Poem I Meant to Write

I. The Last Drive

Driving west to see
You, I stopped
For the sun
And a trooper.
I was flying.
You were
Suddenly, finally gone.
There's a better way
To say this.
The apples you love
Bounced and rolled
Out of their sack.
I thought of writing
This down
And slipping
It to him: how thin
The route north becomes,
How you bring,
I mean brought,
Up nothing sometimes
Twice a night
From the pit of your gut.
I thought of sketching
Out the quills
Of your ribs
On my left
Hand that twitched
For weeks
After I dropped
What you mailed:
Doctors say six weeks.
By for now, 'k? . . .

II. You in the Car

I held your hand
Once. Outside,
Snow and sun
On the road
We drove on,
And neither of us
Cared
To say anything
About noticing. Or
Seemed to. We
Were two people
Holding hands
Along a road thinning
Into farms of silver,
Stacked silos
Filled with wheat.

III. The Present

I've been drinking
Too much. I want to
Hold your hand
As you sip
Red juice
From a blue straw
And click the morphine slow.

IV. The Past

I remember
So many lights
In that hospital
Room that was all yours
Until the end of time,
Your time,
Which I've made
My time because
I feel this way
And that way
For your hands
Thinning. Just your
Hands thinning.

V. Your Wake

What were all those faces
Smiling thinly
At me, not
Asking a thing?
How wet and big
The eyes seemed.
How full and tan
Your cheeks were.
Is this what they mean
By *wake?*

VI. The Future

There's a city somewhere
That opens.
I don't care.
I'm looking
At your letters
Full of snow
And hands and roads.
Everything
Thins and comes
To a point
I try to explain
Away with words
Like *snow* and *thin*
And *hands* and *roads*.
It's easy
To lie here
In this light
Laced with smoke
And jazz and gin.
I'm saying out loud,
I don't care. Listen . . . .
But I still want
To bring you
Green apples
Every day.
More than you
Can eat.

An Elegy for the Living Who Leave

Once, you took my hand
And we coasted
Ireland's shore.
I'm going here . . . .
The map
In your room
Dog-eared, crisp
With sun.
The light smooth
With smoke.
That's all I want
To remember now.
We breathed.
I had given myself up,
And then it was over.
I want to make it
Yesterday
Again. Maybe it is.
What time is it
There? How strong
Am I supposed to be?
Is this a love poem?
Stop listening. Begin
Again. Walking
In the cold
All night,
I tried to think
Of what claims us; clocks
Chimed, ticked, slid
Into somewhere
Else, and snow swirled
Furious tiaras
Around the light

Of the lampposts.
I tried to think
Of what we say
To forget. And that
I remembered.
When I called you
Grasshopper,
Did you think of a lily
Tilting, of an old man
Groaning in his sleep?
I didn't think
Of a thing
And it was full.
Your window
Is not filling
With light
And I don't know
What patience is.
That's why I bother.
That's why I'm here.
You must know
That I am
Scared. And cold.
You're in Dublin.
Have I wished
It were yesterday yet,
Before the falling snow
And your rising flight
Through the snow
That covered and carried
It all to this page?
You're running
To your car,

Singing to the sea,
And there are gulls
Joining you.
This is an elegy
For the living
Who leave.
Now, I'm ahead
Of myself.
This is your laughter.
The memory of it I mean.
The light, I mean,
Not through your window.
I'm staring
There. I'm writing
It's snowing.

III.

Finishing Joyce's *Ulysses* on the Bus,
I Want to Bask in My Sin One More Time

> *Hellenise it.*
> —James Joyce

Above the bus's break squeal, the toddler's
Yelp for love or sleep or milk, his mother's cursing

Prayer for the same, Molly's final *yes* hangs like exhaust.

I close the heavy, Bible-sized book. No need
To save my place anymore with this photo of a woman

I tried to love once. Now, I'm done.

And now a crimson sea slides behind my eyes, and poppies
Bloom, then burn. I have to take it. My stop will come,

Just over the bridge.

Amazing how all things fit into something small
As a day, God's first splintered image, which broke

His heart. Then ours.

*   *

The last time was late spring. She stretched in a sheer white
sundress
Under the lindens and glided my hand

So she might rise, writhe a little, come. *Yes,*

Because we'd given in, again, because it had to be
The last time. And yes, this is the past,

Where ecstasy turns to violation.

But who was it, really, that stretched her veins
Into our borrowed cosmos of grass and shade?

If you say it was me, then I'll tell you

That climax is not epiphany, but an absence of memory, a void
Of image, that there is only one sign that gives birth

To all the others: some dust gathering on her dog-eared
photograph.

Once, this dust cursed its boredom. God loved it,
Felt pity, and slid His finger gingerly inside.

It rose and smiled. But over time, it turned its back on Him.

Desire exiles.

Anyway, it's what this photo tells me.

She's smiling. A blurry close-up: a blue scarf,
A red hat, dark lipstick. Blowing a kiss, it looks

As though she's really waving goodbye.

An orange light, muted, hovers in the back.

Maybe she just finished saying something
About her day or where we had to go or how

The snow just stopped. Something meaningless, beyond cruelty,

Love. No one knows, so I can say anything, almost
Make it true. *Yes.* I could make up our entire lives together,

All the broken china and shattered picture frames of jealousy
Swept into lingering lines, I could try to catch us

In an image of snow, the way a photographer
Hangs up the day's negatives and waits for them to dry,

How she watches the solution's drops fall as she removes
Her rubber gloves, turning them slowly inside out.

And if it were raining outside, I could convince you
That she started singing, and even though she was tone deaf,

She sounded happy, or sincere. Because I think she almost was.

But you do know, don't you? You know that, in truth,
She was a gorgeous sweep of flesh shimmering

For a second or two, not in the grass, but in a hotel room.

And someone else's wife.

Which is why she rose, and mouthed *Yes yes yes*
As she eased slowly back, away, toward the door,

Then closed it.

For My Double Standing Outside Samuel Barber's House, West Chester, Pennsylvania

Degenerate, addict, second cousin,
Stinking of piss and smoke and time,

You're still here, outside Samuel Barber's house waiting
For the streetlights to appear, which are not stars,

Stars that have aligned us with their indifferent agenda.

You're still hoping *Adagio* never ends, but if it does,
Then with a minor fall, guiding you again

Toward the stronger current of a maze I've never seen
Out of, nor want to. It ends, of course, each time
In its minor way, and, like time, is only temporary.

Wind interrupts it, then replaces it. Wind estranges.

Its story used to make me sleepy as it sang
All through that summer when I began to see
How being alone was nothing special,

And unavoidable. I was alone, yes, except,
I had you. You see, an old man

Snored in the lobby, and I kissed her, and wind
Gently rattled through the elevator shaft. Nothing.

This took eight years. So, she and I
Promised never to speak again, unless

It was about the stars and how the sky falls through them.

Because, now, it does. I see it best in summer, when wind
Tricks me into being cool and, momentarily, at ease.

That summer the bricks in the walk started shifting
Beneath my feet, and the cafés filled with friends
Whose faces I couldn't decipher, and flesh burned

And flaked to white dust, and no one said a thing.

To keep safe, I stood in your shadow.

And every interruption of our story was no longer a distraction,
But infinite, beautiful, and without purpose.

There was never a point to the nervous stutters
And polite declinations of the stars that keep the trees in place

And trace the shapes the mourning doves make
With their throats, which mimic their wings.

You know, nothing's changed, ever. It's you
In your ripped pleather jacket standing for the rest of your life

Outside Samuel Barber's house.

You light a match, and your eyes reach
For the Ozarks, or Anchorage, or a rusted side-gate

To heaven, which burns the flesh clean off when it's touched.

You're so gone with Colt .45, sadness,
And some powder wrapped in tinfoil

That I can hear our childhood rustling through the elms.

It sounds like rain at the end of summer,
These airy riffs splicing through each other.

We breathe them in with flame.

St. Johns' Extract

Behind my eyes lately the sun doesn't flash in the river
And this warm wind to my left is finishing off a rock.

Part of the earth spins in the darkness found in a shut
Mouth. There's a stoned girl in the park shaking
A *Crown Royal* bottle with green and black beads in it.

The cashier smiles at me sympathetically, like I'd hoped
She wouldn't as I place it on the counter. We share

An embarrassment teenagers feel in the backs of cars,
But she can't see me turning on my side in bed,
Listening for music at 4 A.M.

The name must be an amalgam of all the St. Johns:
The headless Baptist; the exiled author of *Revelation;*

The father of Peter the Rock; and the John called Mark,
Companion to Paul, crucified upside down—a pair
Of swallows sat on his feet and pecked at the mist

Of gnats congregating around his toes. He moaned
Like you think he'd moan, refusing the sponge

Of vinegar the guard thrust to his mouth. To be in such company
One must remain in good spirits. How could the blessed not be?

Theirs was a pain of the body.

My friend John would pack a bowl at one red light, light it
At the next, and inhale as we merged with the swirl

Of Philadelphia on I-95. He blew his hit in my direction

And I took it in as my own. *Kind of Blue* in the tape deck,
Slouching, sleepy horns. For hours, without comment,

We had visions of every sunny place there was. Now
He's at the Presidio and knows how to kill

Painlessly by snapping the top vertebrae.
That's what they do there; they're good at it.

When he exhales in his bunk at night,
It echoes down the hall before it gets quiet again.

On "Naima," track 6, *Giant Steps*, Coltrane doesn't play
For over half the song. When he does, though, like in the album

Photo, he shuts his eyes tight, as if he were controlled
    by the progression
Rather than controlling it, and the engineer, overwhelmed with bliss
And remorse, excuses himself to call his ex-girlfriend in Kansas City.

That's the story. And as Coltrane empties
His spit valve into the trash can, Jimmy Cobb sets his brushes
Down and says, *Man, St. John Coltrane,*
Please play it, again and again and again . . . .

His eyes stay shut for almost another minute. Behind them,
A blue train stocked with daffodils wanders without sound
Before hiding beneath his memory of the phrases he's just created.

I'm afraid to look, he says, *that's all.*

A Letter to My Friend after Staring at O'Keeffe's
Nothing Is Less Real than Realism

> *Out here, I feel there's something*
> *I've forgotten . . .*
> > —Christopher Buckley

1. The Soul

Dear Chris, I've been thinking about my grandfather,
I've been trying to place his face right in front of mine

Because his name is my name.

I've been staring at bones, blossoms,
The reach of light through a deer's skull,

Black places painted gray and blue drifting
Through a pelvis. In that distance glazed with moon

I can almost make out my bone-smooth soul.

But look here, in this one, O'Keeffe retreats
To language, plain, direct, exact,

Which reminds me that the light
                                        O'Keeffe has conjured is oil.

At least, that's how I imagine it.

Imagining involves belief. Maybe I stare not after my
grandfather,
But because I'd forgotten about the soul. Let me

Imagine it walking up a dusty path at night, a coyote
Thirty paces behind, a rattler poised in the brush;

And when the soul stops to catch its breath,
The coyote sings and the rattler curls around itself

In prayer, counting the beads of its tail.

And what of this stillness descending upon the three of us,
Conceivably from where wind frightens itself?

Is that wind composing the soul,
Or is it the soul's altitude teasing me

Out of memory and into a more intimate blue?

2. A Name

It could be this easy, Chris: because our twenty-six letters

Are darkness, are as fluent as the sky
Reflecting on itself in a puddle showing

Outer space, and beneath the puddle words thrown
Through lungs,

I write my grandfather's name. Nothing seems more real.

Thing is, like you, I can't see him.

But what's a name but an idea standing
For something else, something that stops listening

And stands on its own—

Without a word or nod, it walks out
Of the room where its friends and family go on talking

Over each other, and someone lights a Montecristo

And blows a pillow of smoke
That perhaps resembles the soul's ascension.

But, the name, where does it go?

Maybe it walks, maybe it stirs the sea and shuffles the clouds,
Blasts sand into glass, glass into dust,

Ripples the puddle, shatters its image.

When it thirsts, it makes itself
Heard in a coyote's song, and takes up house

In one of O'Keeffe's bone portals.

If I stare long enough, I can hear the scrape
Of someone writing my name for the first time.

3. The Real

I've heard nothing is real, Chris, nothing.

That's why I stare, now, at this picture that doesn't exist:
My grandfather holding me an hour after I'm born.

That's why O'Keeffe abandoned light
For a few words swept eastward:

Details are confusing.

It is only by selection, by elimination, by emphasis
That we get at the real meaning of things . . .

Saying it doesn't make it so, and
                                    a belief in nothing can mean

Everything the soul won't say. For example,

If the soul accepts its own society,
It does so by rising out of bed; it disconnects

The tubes, it lets the monitor hum its lone piercing note; it leaves
The door slightly ajar,

Which lets a little blue bleed through
From the hospital's farthest corner,

Where a baby's cry circles down the hall.

Still Life with Suicide

Maybe it's worth it: no one dies
More alone, more slowly than the suicide.

They have become their desire, their own admirers, they are no longer
Clichés of our own grief and narcissism.

But why does this poem feel otherwise, why have I placed my friend B.
Inside a still life, the moment before

He looks up at St. Joseph's statue, spits, and kisses

The pistol? No desire, maybe, though this moment has snow
Falling, enough to create a quiet so large that even madness

Seems to descend like a gift, or a song. I don't know
Much about madness, but B. must have practiced it daily

The way a singer will leap through scales backstage
Or in the green room holding a cup of tea.

If B.'s performance was final, his image is not.

That's why I'm here, still.

                        *   *

How selfish the living can be:

At dinner after the funeral, I broke three fingers
Breaking someone's jaw who claimed

That B. was a pussy. How blinding

Grief can be, how selfish and necessary
To blurt it out between shots of Bushmill's and plates of roasted pork.

B. and all the suicides don't have to deal with us anymore; how
Careless of me to lump them all

Together. Dante knew better, but
Still got it wrong. What dreams may come

For them are not suffused with rings of fire,
But are fleshed out in sleep, gauzy canvases of us grieving,

Then forgetting them.

Wind blows through the high windows of the mansion they stay in.

The white curtains sway like wet swans or the mane of a palomino.

B. leans back, curls into himself, and sips some warm milk.

He pulls the white blanket up.

Metaphor

> *One swallow makes a summer*
> —Robert Lowell

Listen B.
      it'll be this
           instead

The freighter trellis
           straddling the Delaware
Is a violin bow and all

The blown trash on all the forgotten
Train platforms
        we pissed on
Are those picturesque French cottages
No one from around here
          ever stays in

The sky will beat its way
        easterly
Even in its Catholic-sweater navy-blue

Even as its own dream stands still
In the gauzy authority of say
          O'Keeffe

The blown shape
        of an hourglass
Has always been infinitely feminine
          and bearable

What were we

thinking

Because you've blindly passed
                                                  into the eye
As dust
            impossibly
                              ecstatic

Lowell is right

Some things are hopeful

                  *   *

We should talk for hours
                                        in pig Latin

Ow-bay
               ash-tray
                               and-stay

Yes
        the Delaware's cartography

Resembles a few snapped horsehairs   **95**
Swaying from the bow

Or a vein expanding
Into a bottomless net
                              of salmon

This is how the world drops
Chief
       into flame

          It doesn't

A Trail of Blue Smoke

I see quick fangs of fire
                from a .22 and a trail of blue smoke

Rising expectedly from the hole B. put in his head

That's beside the point
                The future has yet to reveal itself
As something revisable

The smoke from B.'s mouth could be conceived as immaculate

And so blessed are Busch pounders doused with jiggers of amaretto

They are best drunk outdoors at night
    on an abandoned strip of rail line in December

The only sound
            some stars and wind shuffling leaves
Into a pointless arrangement of the light we had coming

From B.'s chrome zippo and the occasional car turning left

All streets ended
        where our tracks began

When SEPTA shut down that route
            depression rose
As a bad tattoo

There were cars but no more jobs in a town
Where work is the salt sustaining all things

                                                 holy as ash

Bears witness to smoke

Smoke a genuflection
                    to fire
As fire chooses to remain speechless

B. should cup his hand around my face
And hold the blue-hemmed flame to light me up

Poof chief he says *every single time*

The future will never be
                            revisable

Still Life: Eggs in Linen

This is not about what I wanted
To start with, a floor, some sun
Slanting through, turning the amber tiles
Warmer, suddenly, as if someone
Were there sleeping, or waking,
Watching that slowness open
A lily. It's not
About what I've wanted. It is
Only a floor, some light stunned
Upon a lily, and someone
Breathing under a blue blanket.
I am not watching this from a distance
Anymore. How many times
Have I walked through alleys
Kicking a stone curb to curb,
Hands in my pockets, almost warm?
How many times has snow scabbed
The surface of a pond, the koi bashful
And waving beneath? How many times
Have I marked the calendar in blue
Pencil my last days in this man's shape?
This is not about what I want.
The floor is warm, that's all, and not
By its own accord. And that is why
This is not a love poem, why it does not move
Beyond desire, unlike the sun,
From the floor to beneath the blanket,
To wrapping, Sweet Jesus, my cold hands
Around your cold hands, hands that, once,
Drew dots as small as stars
And made silver eggs dimly glow

In some linen-wrapped forever.
It's just paper. It's not
About what I want at all.

Vigil

As it fades with Coltrane riding a high-range C

I am thinking of the body's postures of desire
                                    finite as they are

The most resilient among them composed
                                    of air

This air near the tip of a tongue whistled

Or not yet thought of
                    not yet waved through a horn

Not even missed but unconceived and yet

So much depending
Upon

That air and the guts it takes to ride one note for a minute
Straight if you're a jazz musician

The band behind him working around it
                                    no questions asked

Elvin Jones shuffling his brushes and shrugging at Jimmy
Garrison
    who grins widely over

At McCoy Tyner slumped over his striding wrists
Or is it at the bartender's apparent confusion changing to rage

Scratching his head wiping the bar in the same spot
Breaking glasses on purpose to see if that would shake things
up

Finally scratching his head

                just scratching his head

Not having thought yet of desire embodied as soundlessness

Not like this guy I called Vigil all one summer
Who'd walk the block aligning trash cans

After the workers had thrown them back to the curb

Vigil would stand to view his work mumbling

                        a little

Sometimes whimpering

                sometimes singing to the light
In his fist

Then he'd pace deliberately as a spider weaving a corner
For itself in Copernicus's study

                the story goes

                      whose web he
wanted
To figure into his calculations

Regarding the speedy movement

                    of the star that is
Venus before his cat Christophe hopped in his lap and spilled

His wine all over his notebook

The universe as we might have known it

                    maroon-smeared
Lost and swimming

There are worse things

This was 1532
        the New World taking shape in the form

Of cloves and slaves by the ship-full
                not sailing toward the sky

At the edge of the earth but into it as one might walk
Through a waterfall to find on the other end a cave
Housing snakes and eels
        or a paradise captured

And glossy in the pages of a travel magazine

I leafed through all that summer and found the cost too high
To go anywhere that offered a view of Eden or Costa Rica

And room service for a week

So I stayed put walked around the neighborhood
At dawn most of the time
           sky sheer as a peach blouse

And just as thick
        erasure moon   starlings   sparrows

And Vigil
        walking up and down the block with houses

That looked painted in around him
          and his arrangement

Of some fifteen cans lined side-by-side

                                                  or stacked pyramidic
Or set down like a cord of wood

After he'd get them right the owners of the cans
Would drag them back home

                                    some cursing

                                                    some laughing

Some whistling all the way home and up the driveway

A tune they might not be able to name

                                                but still

A tune engrained so they come back

                                        whoever

Standing in the doorway tall and straight

Because of a note that is puckered and blown

So high
            it holds

photo by Marina Fedosik

Alexander Long was born and raised in Sharon Hill, Pennsylvania. He's worked as a musician, fry cook, and obituary writer. With Christopher Buckley, he is co-editor of *A Condition of the Spirit: the Life & Work of Larry Levis* (Eastern Washington University Press, 2004). His poems, essays, and book reviews have appeared in *American Writers* (Charles Scribner's Sons), *Blackbird, The Cream City Review, 5 AM, Pleiades, Poetry International, The Prose Poem: An International Journal, Quarter After Eight, Quarterly West, Rivendell, Solo, Third Coast*, and elsewhere. He is a member of the writing faculty at West Chester University and writes, plays, and tours with the band Redhead Betty Takeout.

New Issues Poetry

Vito Aiuto, *Self-Portrait as Jerry Quarry*
James Armstrong, *Monument in a Summer Hat*
Claire Bateman, *Clumsy, Leap*
Kevin Boyle, *A Home for Wayward Girls*
Michael Burkard, *Pennsylvania Collection Agency*
Christopher Bursk, *Ovid at Fifteen*
Anthony Butts, *Fifth Season, Little Low Heaven*
Kevin Cantwell, *Something Black in the Green Part of Your Eye*
Gladys Cardiff, *A Bare Unpainted Table*
Kevin Clark, *In the Evening of No Warning*
Cynie Cory, *American Girl*
Peter Covino, *Cut Off the Ears of Winter*
James D'Agostino, *Nude with* Anything
Jim Daniels, *Night with Drive-By Shooting Stars*
Joseph Featherstone, *Brace's Cove*
Lisa Fishman, *The Deep Heart's Core Is a Suitcase*
Robert Grunst, *The Smallest Bird in North America*
Paul Guest, *The Resurrection of the Body and the Ruin of the World*
Robert Haight, *Emergences and Spinner Falls*
Mark Halperin, *Time as Distance*
Myronn Hardy, *Approaching the Center*
Brian Henry, *Graft*
Edward Haworth Hoeppner, *Rain Through High Windows*
Cynthia Hogue, *Flux*
Joan Houlihan, *The Mending Worm*
Christine Hume, *Alaskaphrenia*
Josie Kearns, *New Numbers*
David Keplinger, *The Clearing, The Prayers of Others*
Maurice Kilwein Guevara, *Autobiography of So-and-So: Poems in Prose*
Ruth Ellen Kocher, *When the Moon Knows You're Wandering,*
        One Girl Babylon
Gerry LaFemina, *Window Facing Winter*
Steve Langan, *Freezing*

Lance Larsen, *Erasable Walls*
David Dodd Lee, *Abrupt Rural, Downsides of Fish Culture*
M.L. Liebler, *The Moon a Box*
Alexander Long, *Vigil*
Deanne Lundin, *The Ginseng Hunter's Notebook*
Barbara Maloutas, *In a Combination of Practices*
Joy Manesiotis, *They Sing to Her Bones*
Sarah Mangold, *Household Mechanics*
Gail Martin, *The Hourglass Heart*
David Marlatt, *A Hog Slaughtering Woman*
Louise Mathias, *Lark Apprentice*
Gretchen Mattox, *Buddha Box, Goodnight Architecture*
Lydia Melvin, *South of Here*
Carrie McGath, *Small Murders*
Paula McLain, *Less of Her; Stumble, Gorgeous*
Sarah Messer, *Bandit Letters*
Wayne Miller, *Only the Senses Sleep*
Malena Mörling, *Ocean Avenue*
Julie Moulds, *The Woman with a Cubed Head*
Marsha de la O, *Black Hope*
C. Mikal Oness, *Water Becomes Bone*
Bradley Paul, *The Obvious*
Katie Peterson, *This One Tree*
Elizabeth Powell, *The Republic of Self*
Margaret Rabb, *Granite Dives*
Rebecca Reynolds, *Daughter of the Hangnail, The Bovine Two-Step*
Martha Rhodes, *Perfect Disappearance*
Beth Roberts, *Brief Moral History in Blue*
John Rybicki, *Traveling at High Speeds* (expanded second edition)
Mary Ann Samyn, *Inside the Yellow Dress, Purr*
Ever Saskya, *The Porch is a Journey Different From the House*
Mark Scott, *Tactile Values*
Hugh Seidman, *Somebody Stand Up and Sing*
Martha Serpas, *Côte Blanche*
Diane Seuss-Brakeman, *It Blows You Hollow*
Elaine Sexton, *Sleuth*